SOL SATISFACTION

Scott Kelsey

Scott Kelsey: Sol Satisfaction

Copyright 2022

Print ISBN 978-1-66784-956-0
eBook ISBN 978-1-66784-957-7

DEDICATION

Dedicated to my family. My wife, Lynda. My son,
Nathan. My daughter, Peri and my mother, Jane.

ACKNOWLEDGMENTS

I have now spent a good majority of my life in
Cecil County, at the head of the Chesapeake Bay. I
have always been drawn to water. The next part of
the journey will continue near the Atlantic Ocean
and the back bays of Delaware and Maryland.

CONTENTS

DEDICATION   V

ACKNOWLEDGMENTS   VII

CHAPTER 1 DELMARVA   1

    Dune Grass, Fenwick, DE   2

    East 54   3

    Keydash, Isle of Wright Bay   5

    A Lone Duck, On a Lake,

    The Lenape Indian Crossed Here   6

    Eastern Shore, Winter Morning   7

    Have You Seen, The Sun Rise

    Over the Atlantic Ocean?   8

    Summertime Sunday with Lynda   9

    100 Years Ago, Today   10

    Watch September   11

    Moving Fast, Going Slow   12

    Autumn Sky   13

    The Day, After The Day (Family)   14

    Thankful   16

    Fall Rain   17

    Simple Life (Carbon Footprint)   18

    December the Defiant   19

    January   21

    The Season   22

    Bone on Bone   24

    Dead Calm Reflecting   25

    Summer   26

CHAPTER 2 HOPE   27

    Who Will Save the World?   28

    What If   29

    Someday/Sunday/Hope   30

Friday, June 5th (Take a breath)   31

Gingerly   32

Twilights Last Gleaming   33

Lay Me Down   35

For You   37

Left and Right   38

9/11   39

Outside The Circle   40

Aprils Journey   41

CHAPTER 3 FAMILY   43

Déjà vu   44

A Saturday in Spring (for Pete)   45

Petey, Man's Best Friend   46

Farmers' Almanac   48

I Can See Your Beard From Here   49

JH   50

Dancing Under a Midnight Sky – 5.2.19   52

Pirates and Cowboys Only Worry About Today   55

Old Ford Pickup   57

Birthday For a Friend   58

CHAPTER 4 NATURE   59

Solid I Stand   60

Solitude Standing   61

Venus   63

The Dark Comes Through Us   64

There Are No Bad Days When You're Fishing   65

The Lightning Bugs Will Emerge   67

Spiraling Equinox   69

Mind Full   70

Landlocked Sailing   71

A New Day   72

October Fishing, A Full Moon   73

Wanderlust   75

Winter, Wind Chill   76

Swirls of Light   77

Sleeping Under the Stars   78

Elements   79

Planet Earth From the Moon   80

Friday Night   82

CHAPTER 5 MISCELLANEOUS   83

Sunday's Pondering over a Cup of Coffee   84

Untitled   86

Back in the Day...Tonight   87

The Silence Goes Unheard   88

Stay (a) Home   90

Late Last Night   92

'Round Here   93

There's a Hole in Daddy's Heart

(homage to John Prine)   94

Springtime C=19 2020   97

Quarantine With Edgar Allen Poe's Ghost   98

C=19   100

The New World (Jack Kerouac's, On the Road)   102

39°38'17.5"N 75°57'45.2"W   103

Maya   104

Library   105

Bones and Blood   107

Objects May Appear Larger   108

On the Road to Kathmandu   109

Pirates   110

Love   112

The Summer is Not Over   113

Mother/Daughter   114

A Nation is Born   115

Anywhere USA   116
Step Outside, Tonight (homage to NASA,
Neil Armstrong, and Astronauts)   117
Do Not Wish; Do   118
Notre-Dame de Paris   120
The Dimming of Democracy   122
State of Mind/Between the Two/A Love Story   123
Eugene Martin's Last Day in the Low Country   124

CHAPTER 1

DELMARVA

Dune Grass, Fenwick, DE

Footprints,
And tan lines,
Slowly fade,
Walking on the beach,
The Summer Sun,
Begins to Fall,
Bare feet or Flip-flops,
Walking on the beach,
The hustle and bustle,
Of Summer,
Finally breaks,
Walking on the beach,
Like a good book,
Almost finished,
We count the pages,
Sitting on the beach,
A flannel shirt,
A pair of cutoffs,
A beach chair,
Sitting on the beach,
No more people watching,
Now I watch the waves,
Uninterrupted,
Today on the beach,
The Summer memories,
Still linger,
In a year forgotten,
Today on the beach.

There is a road leading to a rising sun,
A road traveled,
A road filled with,
Potholes,
Bumps,
Curves,
Dead Ends,
Detours,
Crashes,
Fender Benders,
Scrapes and Scars,

A road traveled,
A road filled with,
Late nights,
Early mornings,
Broken hearts,
Broken bones,
Broken pavement,
Broken promises,

A road traveled,
A road filled with,
Chemicals,
and false hopes,
A road filled with,
Regrets,
Tears,
Fears,
And a few beers,

East on 54,
To the sun,
to the home,
and then some,

East on 54,
To a calm,
To a peace,
To sand,
To surf,
To love,
To anew,
East on 54,
To you.

Keydash, Isle of Wright Bay

4:00 am,
80 degrees,
100% humidity,
Cicadas are singing,
The fishing boat starts,
Spudders and comes to life,
So, do I,
The moon fears the morning,
The stars steer me,
My heart pounds,
As I drive in dark water,
Seagulls are still dreaming,
Buoys blink awake,
She sits up front on the Yeti,
Shorts,
A teal blue tee shirt, 1967 Haight-Ashbury,
and her favorite flip-flops,
I have a coffee cup in my hand,
Steering with the other,
She has her fishing rod ready,
Spotting our first fishing spot,
I turn off the engine,
Far enough out of the cove to glide in,
We never talk,
Just a nautical/marine dance,
You can't see,
Just hear a splash, in front of the boat,
The fish have been feeding by moonlight,
She casts in the dark, before
the boat comes to a stop,
Throwing lures along the shoreline,
I sip coffee,
and listen to the daybreak,
For a moment there is peace,
There is calm.

A Lone Duck, On a Lake,
The Lenape Indian Crossed Here
•••••••••••••••••••••••••••

The silence swirls,
With the almost Autumn trees,
Mirrored are the colors of Fall,
The Lenape crossed this way,
A part of the Algonquin tribe,
Deer, fish, and fowl,
They followed,
The trail among the salt marshes,
And Tidal wetlands,
Running South and East,
The gray sky blends into the corn fields,
Wilting on the stalk,
Soybeans are still a ways off from harvest,
Holding onto their Summer green,
I watch a lone duck,
On a Lake,
Floating with the wind,
As my mind wanders.

Eastern Shore, Winter Morning

A dawn walk,
It is cold,
The wind,
Brisk,
Coffee is the only option,
Snow and Canadian Geese,
Fly above,
In chaotic V's,
Up from the ponds and the lakes,
Looking for fields,
Corn or soybeans,
Emptied a month before,
Combined and cleared,
Except for the stalk and,
Stray ears or pods,
They fill fields,
And seem content,
I am,
On this morning walk.

And 60 years have passed,
Pretending the world would not fall apart,
Flowing along with the tide,
Playing with the moon,
Shining with the sun,
Drinking in the human soul,
From a distance,
I watched,
As people performed,
Their dance of the ignorantly bliss,
And wondered about my children's children,
The simple task,
Of walking barefoot on the morning grass,
On the sand,
As it cools off on a summer's evening,
When did we take for granted what is before us,
As pieces of the world crumple,
Pieces of the puzzle go missing,
Parts of the human race melt away,
Blood and bodies,
Politics and passions,
People and places,
Fade, like the memory of your youth,
And 60 years have passed,
Pretending the world, will not fall apart,
Wishing the world, can heal,
Hoping the world, can find love,
Praying the world can get me to 61.

Summertime Sunday with Lynda

Water and our soul
Waves ripple or
Waves roar
I'm standing next to you
Two feet off the floor
You lean to kiss me
We wash upon the shore
Water and our soul
Washed with salt and sun
Tan lines
Flip flop tan
Bathing suit tan
Tan lines of your sunglasses
Cotton ball white
With hues of blue sky
Water in our soul
You lean to kiss me
Salt on your lips
Fire in your fingertips
Sand between our toes
We are in Summer
And so, it goes.

100 Years Ago, Today

Snow geese fly south,
Talking to each other,
Along the way,
They look for corn fields,
Finished for the season,
Cut and combined,
The fields,
Once plentiful,
Taken over by "progress",
Sold for retirement money,
Fade as fast as the Winter Sun,
The Farmer,
Still makes a living,

Watch September

There are still footprints in the sand,
Unwashed by the ocean,
Still leaves on the trees,
They have yet to fall into motion,
There are still tomatoes,
Ripe on the vine,
Still Summer,
Still time,
There are geese,
Landing in harvested fields,
There are hot days,
And cool damp nights,
There is still time for flip-flops and sunshine,
There are bonfires and moonshine,
I hear summer songs on the radio,
There is still a lot of grass to mow,
Look for apples ready by the bushel,
Summer is lost and fall is official.

Moving Fast, Going Slow

August,
And its corn,
Sweet,
Tomatoes,
Ripe and red,
Mayo,
White bread,

August,
And the rain came,
After Sun drenched days,
Soaking the ground,
Refreshing the air,
Replenishing,

August,
Ending Summer,
For some,
Labor Day weekend,
The setting sun.

Autumn Sky

We came here long ago,
The flame in the Autumn sky,
Dancing shadows in the moonlight,
Some say crazy,
A little insane,
Outside,
The rain,
A Hurricane,
October into,
November,
When's the last time we watched the leaves fall,
I can't remember,
The wind blows,
Cold into the bone,
A good day for hot coffee,
And a fire, at home,
Trees have the weight of the Season,
Laying on their limbs,
We'd jump in all the puddles,
But then we must learn how to swim,
The tomatoes are rotting on the vine,
The green peppers too,
The corn has been harvested,
Pumpkins still sit,
In the morning dew.

The Day, After The Day (Family)

The water on the bay,
Reflects the chill,
A light fog,
The tide stands still,
The cormorant and loon,
Sense the morning mood,
My fishing rod has crystals forming on it,
My feet are numb, like my shoes don't fit,
We had pizza with popcorn as a dessert,
For Thanksgiving dinner last night,
There was no family in sight,
This morning,
On the water,
Looking for some Rockfish filets,
Oysters by the dozen,
Life's okay,
There's coffee brewing back home,
There's a fire in the fireplace,
There's a pandemic and the great unknown,
There's hours and hours of the unseen,
There's the blonde lady by my side,
through thick and thin,
We jump in the truck another journey begins,
Her cold nose and a warm kiss,
It's the whole family,
Together,
That I miss,
On into December and the New Year,
Will there be merriment and good cheer,
The rush of the future,
Life's okay,
There's a pandemic and the great unknown,

There're waves crashing at the ocean,
There's revolution put in motion,
Our family's footprint(s) in the sand,
We will be here to lend a hand,
Perspective and the positive,
We look to the summer,
Cold beer and sunshine,
This morning,
The bay, the ocean and Life,
Hopefully, will look fine.

Thankful
· · · · · · · ·

Wake up to blue sky
Lost in a meadow of dreams
Fog lifts
Listen to the gentle stream
A deer grazes nearby
A fire burns
Your heart
And soul
And we still have concerns
You drink wine
Beer by the glass
Help me up when I fall
    You're the saltwater healing
    That feeling
    You are living
    Have a happy
Thanksgiving.

Fall Rain
• • • • • • • •

A of coffee cup,
    Sends,
        Contrails of warmth,
Vapor,
          Evaporates,
Outside,
    The Rain
        Falls,
The tin roof,
    Echos the sound,
        Patting, Pat,
Pat,
The fireplace,
 Crackles,
  With an occasional,
               Pop,
A nap is in order,
    Outside,
    The Rain,
Falls.

Simple Life (Carbon Footprint)

His old bones,
Have found a home,
Among the Salt and Sand,
There are scars on his body,
Lines on his hands,
Gnarled by Earth,
Worked by the Land,

The sights he sees,
The air he breathes,
Now comes from the Ocean,
Down to the Sea,

He lives there peacefully,
The sound of the waves,
The Summer breeze,
Eyes with crow's feet,
A smile when you meet,

His old bones,
Have found a home,
Among the grass and dunes,
His heart is weaker now,
Though his spirit still improves,
With the warmth of Sun,
And winter solitude,
His old bones have found a home.

December the Defiant

The geese leave the cornfields,
Just as the sun goes down,
Looking for water,
Protection,
Shotgun's unload,
Off in the distance,
I saw a coyote today,
Running through the fields,
The sky is on fire,
Just above the horizon,
Deer feed right at the wood line,
Until dark,
December is a survival month,
The end of a year,
Rain mixes with snow,
Wind mixes with cold,
Bones feel the weather,
We begin to feel the old,
How do the trees survive?
Naked, raw,
Exposed,
Dormant,
Only to come alive in a few months,
If we can make it those few months,
I take the boat south,
In my mind,
The Outer Banks,
Emerald Isle,
Kiawah Island,
Tybee Island,
The Low Country,
In search of sun,

Surf fishing,
A chance for flip-flops,
In my mind,
I watch the sunrise a thousand times,
I feel its warmth,
Only a few months,
December is an old month,
Ahead of us is something new.

January
· · · · · · ·

There's a cell tower,
Off in the foggy distance,
The light on top,
Blinks on,
Blinks off,
Blinks on,
Blinks off,

The rain continues,
Drip,
Drip,
Drip,
Drip,
Pattering on the porch,

January is a dreary month,
Filled with grays and gloom,
Christmas trees, tossed aside,
Sugar and sweets consumed,

Decorations done,
We search,
We search,
For the midnight Sun.

The Season
·········

The sand,
At your feet,
Sticks like snow and sleet,
On a winter's day,
Footprints,
In the frozen dew,
Angels and stars,
Fly and fall,
Way to far,
Inside,
You,
The tide,
Moves,
Like rain,
On a rainy day,
Outside,
You,
The tears move,
Down your cheeks,
Trickling into the ocean,
Your emotions,
Set into motion,
The family,
That won't be around,
No festive sound,
Only an empty echo,
The presence,
Of no presents,
Just the twinkle of a star,
Atop the tree,
For dreaming,
And dreams to see,

On Christmas,
Or Christmas Eve,
So those of you that can be,
With your family,
Hug and Kisses,
Should abound,
The Christmas,
The festive sound,
Should come from your heart,
At least it will be a very good start,
Inside you,
The spirit and feeling,
Of family and healing,
Of a Christmas light,
That they will be with you,
Tonight,
Although nowhere in sight,
The Christmas Spirit,
Is bright,
Peace and love,
On this wondrous night.

Bone on Bone

It's good to have the sun shining on my face,
During this cold morning walk,
The wind is down,
The geese are trying to build up courage,
To unzip their down coats,
The Ocean today,
Is angry,
The clouds,
Want to form a gloom,
Still,
The sand is holding onto a warmth,
Left over from the Summer,
Salt and Sea,
Heal the soul,
I am cold but content,
The sun peeks through,
Just enough,
To shine on me,
And throw diamonds on the water,
Bone on bone,
The miles,
On the beach,
Seems so easy.

Dead Calm Reflecting
· · · · · · · · · · · · · · · · ·

The slight hint of creosote,
Gas and Diesel,
Around the piers,
The docks,
Marinas,
Brackish water,
Going a little south,
Salt water,
The Bay,
Off in the distance,
Reggae playing,
Sunshine,
Storms,
Early morning fog, mist,
Looking at the weather,
Checking the weather,
Thinking about the tide,
Iced down beer in the cooler,
Heat,
Humidity,
Sweat,
The scent of suntan lotion,
A dip into the water,
A dip in time,
A vacation,
A weekend,
A day,
Moments,
On the Chesapeake Bay.

Summer

· · · · · ·

Summer,
Through sunglasses,
Shorts,
Flip flops,
Your favorite tee-shirt,

The smell of honeysuckle,
Mock Orange,
The scent of coconut,
In the air,

Late night drives,
With the windows down,
The music up,
A smile, on your face,

It's a walk on a forest trail,
After a rainstorm,
The colors come alive,
And so, do you,

A paperback on the beach,
Stained pages,
Sand in between,
Your feet and the world,

It's a boat ride to nowhere,
With no cares,
The warm water,
The salt-air,

Summer, through sunglasses,
Relax when you can,
Work if you must,
Love the people you are with.

CHAPTER 2

Hope

Who Will Save the World?

Was the sunset beautiful there,
Did you have time to see it,
Do you really care,
Were you a little too high today,
Or a little too low,
Did you finish way above?
Or too far below,
Did you get healed,
Did they fix what ails you,
You still have plenty of time,
To see the sights,
To walk the new ground,
To see the world,
Hear the sounds,
I called you today,
There was no answer,
They say the Native American Indians,
Danced with the lightning,
Ran with the wind,
I called today,
When will I see you again,
There is a big world out there,
But we are not small,
We will get through it,
We will get through it all,
There is dark,
That can bring us down,
There is light,
That can be found,
Who will save us,
Who will save the world?
You, will save us,
As sure as the world is round,
And all this love abounds.

What If
. . . . . .

What if,
You could wake up tomorrow,
To love,
To peace,
To good health,
To a world,
Filled with the morning SUN,
A world,
Fill with a billion stars.

Someday/Sunday/Hope

This ship,
She's a sinking,
Got me thinking,
I'm a little too wired,
Tired,
To start day drinking,
Mask over my mouth,
Knee to my throat,
Riot,
Not so quiet,
Burnt up,
Burnt out,
Tomorrow,
Yesterday,
Today,
This morning,
Tonight,
Good night,
We can try again tomorrow.

Friday, June 5th (Take a breath)
. . . .

In the aftermath of rain and storm,
You open the window to your soul,
You react to what is in your heart,
The in between of right and wrong,
Look deep my friend,
That is not a question,
That is the answer.

Gingerly
· · · · · · · ·

I hear the complaints,
About politics,
And all you Saints,
You tell me you can't quite believe,
What you are hearing,
What you see,
All this stuff that is going down,
Getting caught up,
In what is going around,
Take time,
Time again,
And look at who,
Who is sitting next to you,
And who you want sitting next to you,
It's a game of chance we play,
Going outside every day,
Looking out the window,
We must live,
The life we have,
The future,
The past,
The ones you love,
The ones you mourn,
The sun will rise,
The sun will set,
Have you hugged,
The one you love, yet?

Twilights Last Gleaming

Are we broken?
Divided?
Who's thinking?
Who's decided?
Blood red,
Blue and white,
She wears the stripes,
Like falling stars at night,
"We the People,
Of the United States,
In order to form a more perfect union,
Establish justice,
Insure domestic tranquility,"
Outside this house,
We fly the flag,
Proudly,
We are not ignorantly bliss,
To today,
The past,
Or tomorrow,
But with the understanding,
That we are free,
Free,
To voice opinions,
Beliefs,
Religions,
And free,
To stand up,
To the wrong,
For our rights,
It's a fine line,
That we are walking now,

Isn't it?
Freedom and the flag,
A symbol,
Of us,
Of the US,
Of ONE country,
Are we broken?
Divided?
Who's thinking?
Who's decided?
Blood red,
Blue and white,
She wears the stripes,
Like falling stars at night.

Lay Me Down

I just want to lay down,
And leave this world behind,
I just want to go down,
To the place I have in mind,
It's too distracting,
Nerve wracking,
This society of mankind,
Where'd we go before of all this,
We come to know,
Down to the beach,
To the mountains,
To walk in fresh snow,

I just want to lay down,
And watch the blue sky turn to stars,
I want to close my eyes for a while,
And wake up with a smile,
End up,
On Jupiter or Mars,
Ah, to laugh again,
To take the boat down the Bay,
To turn the stereo up,
Way past eleven,
To drown out all the excess noise,
I want to go out west,
And ride the land,
With only the worry of the cowboys,

I want to try,
Maybe fail,
Fall 1,000 times,
To get up one more,
I just want the world to be whole again,
Pure and pristine,
Like it was,
Way back when,
When the sun was shining,
To start over,
And begin,

I just want to lay down,
And shut my eyes for a little bit,
To dream of the future,
For our children's benefit,
I want to take my chances,
In the middle of a hurricane,
Just to make sure I am crazy,
and not too sane,

I want to lay down,
And wake up bathed in morning light,
I want the gray to be gone,
I want you to return to my sight.

For You
· · · · · · ·

Simply,
Breathe,
A deep breath in,
A slow exhale,
Get rid of the anxiety,
Stress,
Negativism,
Turn off the TV,
Radio,
Social Media,
Inhale a breath of fresh air,
It is a mad world,
Meditate for a second,
Pray, if that is your thing,
Stretch your body,
Relax your muscles,
Think of one positive thing,
One thought,
Give yourself a little bit of time,
Each day,
Each day is a new beginning,
Simply,
Breathe.

There's a dark cloud,
Off in the horizon,
On top of me,
Like the weight,
of summer's humidity,
Oppressive,
Soul draining,
There is a dark cloud,
Covering,
The silent,
The singers,
Those that choose,
Those that do not,
Those that have a voice,
Those that do not,
Those that do not want to fight,
Their neighbors,
Their friends,
Their family,
Their foes,
Those that do,
There is a dark cloud,
Dividing as it goes,
This place,
Consumed,
Engulfed,
Inflamed,
Enraged,
Against one another,
There is a dark cloud,
Following,
Off in the distance,
Now upon us.

9/11
• • •

Leaving now,
To watch the sun through the smoke and clouds,
The television plays the wreckage,
Seeing now,
The surface of the moon,
With papers and bodies being strewn,
Being now,
In places you never wanted to be in life,
Responding now,
To the destruction of families,
Firefighters, police, and life,
Losing now,
The piece of what America once was,
Lungs filled now,
With the devil and dust of terrorist,
Running now,
With no place to go,
Except away from the madness and broken,
Falling now,
When what is left is sorrow and sadness,
Remembering now,
That memory that cannot be forgotten.

Outside The Circle
· · · · · · · · · · · · · · · ·

Outside,
The world is burning,
Gone dark,
But there is a spark,
In the heart of the world,
The rising of a new day,
To follow the ray,
Of hope,
A way to cope,
To get by,
Jesus Christ died,
A cross we have to bear,
We now sit in the house,
And go nowhere,
To be fair.

Aprils Journey

Things are looking inward now,
The soul and saints are rising now,
Towards the endless flow,
Of fast and slow,
The body and the blood,
The kindness of letting go.

CHAPTER 3

Family

Déjà vu
. . . . . .

I had this feeling,
Last time,
Like Deja Vu,
My father,
My son,
We were sitting on the back porch,
A couple of beers in hand,
My father,
My son,
In the house,
Music was playing,
The TV was turned down,
Football was on,
We didn't say much,
We didn't have to,
My father,
My son,
I'd like to say things like:
"It will be okay,
I love you,
I am proud of you,
How are you feeling?"
It is also implied,
Peeling the label,
Off a Miller Lite,
Staring out at the water,
Asking about the weather,
Talking about cars,
I think we know,
A father's intuition,
I get up and say,
"Want another beer?"
My father,
My son.

A Saturday in Spring (for Pete)

I walk down an empty lane,
Try and remember,
Sun up,
To sundown,
Like red embers,
Shadows and ghost,
Lingering,
There is heartache,
For the simplest of reasons,
Stumbling along,
A walk in four seasons.

Petey, Man's Best Friend

I walked down the lane tonight,
You seemed to be by my side,

Your house,
And you are not home,

An empty bowl,
Water undrank,
We wait for a bark,
The wag of your tail,

A house,
And you are not home,

You loved us,
Through thick and thin,
In the morning,
There you were,
Every day,
Not mad,
Not sad,
Always happy,

A house,
And you are not home,

You begged for treats,
Popcorn,
Your favorite,

Unconditional Love,

A house,
And you are not home,

You waited at the window,
For our return,

Slept on our bed,
You thought we didn't know,

A house,
And you are not home,

At Christmas, Thanksgiving,
Birthdays, Holidays,
You searched for morsels,
Scraps,
Fallen food,
Napkins, unprotected,

Our house,
And you're not home,

In the last days,
You knew,
You spent time with us,
Looking for a nice neck scratch,
A hug,
Some time,
Some more time,

Our house,
And you are not home,

We miss you,
Only a day gone,
Our house,
And you are not home,

I will walk down the lane,
You by my side,
I will feel you next to me,

A house,
Always your home.

Farmers' Almanac
● ● ● ● ● ● ● ● ● ● ● ● ● ●

They sit,
At the kitchen table,
Grandpa and Grandma,
With biscuits and red eye gravy,
Coffee,
And talk about the weather,
Impending snow,
Wind,
and cold,
They talk about planting crops,
They raised two girls,
On a post-depression farm,
One went to Washington D.C.,
The other Nashville, Tennessee,
They all picked cotton,
By hand,
Bleeding,
Scrimping,
Surviving,
On the earth,
The ground,
The land,
Making quilts,
and
Cutting wood,
For warmth,
For the winter.

I Can See Your Beard From Here

There's a note,
Never spoken,
There's a heart,
Never broken,
There's no reason,
For this season,
Of uncomfortable cold,
That lingers,
In your fingers,

There's a drug,
Never taken,
There's a pain,
Never mistaken,
There's no reason,
For this freezing,
That takes its toll,
Down in my soul,

There's a song,
Never played,
There's a breath,
Never delayed,
There's no reason,
For this cancerous treason,
You have the strength of one million men,
To get back to the beginning and begin again.

There are always voices,
Elevators,
From the ceilings,
Behind closed doors,
Patients,
Parents,
Mothers,
Fathers,
Sisters,
Brothers,
Doctors,
Nurses,
Receptionist,
Stale coffee,
And the silent hum of the lights,
Soothing paintings on the walls,
Antiseptic scents,
Bodies,
Missing pieces,
Missing parts,
Slightly flawed,
Not functioning,
Quite right,
Just a little bit off,
To the left,
Maybe not quite right,
Yet,
And yet,
Everyone here,
Is resilient,
Has hope,
Wants to live,

One more day,
Year,
Years,
And we wait,
The waiting,
To hear,
Something,
Anything,
Positive,
A prognosis,
People,
Are,
Resilient.

I cried,
Wailed,
Just out of earshot,
Just out of the ICU,
Just one year ago, today,
Then I dried my tears,
A lifetime,

You,
In your post-operative,
Drug induced sleep,
Your dreams,
Of running,
Of hiking up the mountain,
When awake,
A metaphor for freedom,

When awake,
Not "I can't",
But when,
Time waits for you,
Just around the corner,
In the shadow,
You are not just another man,
With responsibilities and dreams,
But a lifetime,

You began the climb,
One year ago, today,
A journey to the heavens,
Back to the normal,

You rustle in your sleep,
Dreams of,

Taking steps,
Two steps at a time,
Taking stairs,
To the stars,
Walking,
Down the aisle,

A lesser man wilts in the sun,
Melting into the background,
Hiding from the day,
Not you,
Just another obstacle to figure out,
Just another day to begin,

I held my breath for one year,
Today,
And still,
You have just begun,
The climb,

You rustle in your sleep,
Holding back the darkness,
While you climb,
One step,
Over a rock,
A root,
A mountain,

You rustle in your sleep,
A dream,
A nightmare,
A beginning,
A choice,
To sink,
Your choice,
To swim,

When the negative crept in,
You beat it down,
And beat it,

I rustled in my sleep,
Holding on,
While the wave of emotion tried to push me under,
Never letting go,

You were so positive,
And accepting,
And courageous,
And took one step,
In time,
Past the morning,
Past the mid-day,
Evening,
Night,
Midnight,

A dream,
A reality,
And you continue the climb.

She's got Dreams to go with his regrets,
They smoked dope, instead of cigarettes,
She says go, don't ever surrender,
I looked your way you became my defender,
Turned me down,
You turned me up,
I took a left turn,
U turned again,
Our turn was never luck,

She's shouting now,
The words to a song,
There's no singing,
She's got the lyrics wrong,
Mustang Sally,
Rock and Roll,
The real America's got so much soul,
She don't care about carrying a tune,
She just drinks a beer,
And howls at the moon,

Drove to the mountains,
On a Fall chilly day,
Windows down,
Was the only way,
Drove to the beach,
On a Fall chilly day,
Windows down along the way,

Drove through the darkness,
"Radio does play,
A little Roy Orbison..."
Night turns into day,

They got dreams to go with their regrets,
They smoked dope, instead of cigarettes,
Way out on the shadowed limb,
They forget all the promises,
Fought all the sins,
Sunbeams dance on their thoughts for tomorrow,
Like autumn leaves falling to the ground,
With no regrets, there is no sorrow,
Like autumn leaves falling,
On this Fall chilly day,
There is no sound,
Nothing to say.

Old Ford Pickup
· · · · · · · · · · · · ·

AM radio,
Air condition,
Roll down the windows,
It's got three on the tree,
Clutch that might,
or might not work,
Rust is holding her together,
Memories keep her going,
Granddad chewed tobacco,
Drank whiskey out of a bottle,
Carted cotton,
To market,
Taught me to drive that Ford,
On the farm in the back forty,
Let me drive to the Piggly Wiggly,
Even though I was only fourteen,
When I wasn't driving,
I would sit on the tailgate,
While he drives us around,
Made a game out of dragging our toes on the ground,
The old Ford,
It's two tone and rust,
Made the best,
For all of us.

Birthday For a Friend
· · · · · · · · · · · · · · · · · ·

There's a light,
Always shining,
The Sun,
The Moon,
The smile,
The innocence,
The nicety,
The friendship,
The love,
There is light,
In your heart,
You are pure,
As a sunbeam,
Coming through,
Our cloudy world,
You are you,
Perfect in your own way.

CHAPTER 4

Nature

Solid I Stand

The oak tree fell today,
Plus 100 years from yesterday,
Casting shade,
On the old farmhouse,

Swaying in only the strongest of gusts,
Standing tall,
Dignified,
Strong,

Roots,
That ran,
and rang,
True,

What have you seen,
What have you endured,
Still full of life,
And living,

The tire rope swing,
Picnics on Sundays,
Summer parties,
And Winter winds,

A man came today,
And before I could say goodbye,
Ended you,
Nothing was said, I heard you cry,

The oak tree fell today,
Plus 100 years, from yesterday,
Leaves now float around and around,
One less tree, gone to ground.

Solitude Standing
● ● ● ● ● ● ● ● ● ● ● ● ● ● ● ●

The River to the Bay is quiet now,
There is a peacefulness,
A calm,
Solitude,
But only for the person looking for Solitude,

The Osprey is busy,
Building the nest,
Back and forth with twigs and bits,

The Herron silently stalks its next meal,
Patiently stepping,
Searching,
Scanning,

A Canadian Goose sits on her nest,
Dauntless,
Through the cold,
The rain,
The heat,

Sitting here on the dock,
From the River to the Bay,
There is solitude,
Calm,
A ripple on the water,

There is a Waterman,
Off in the distance,
Catfish, I suppose,
The white rust of his boat,
It used to be a Pratt or Gestewitz,
Out there,
Working for a living,

The sun is hiding behind the gray,
Not quite ready for Summer,
Still holding onto Spring,
The rain has come for 40 days,
I reach for my coffee,
And take one last look,
From the River to the Bay.

Venus
· · · · ·

A lone star,
Shining in the twilight,
Against the dark,
The dark blue,
The shadow light,

Planes dot the sky,
Flashing red in the night,
Contrails,
Trail,
People leaving,
Watching till,
They are out of sight.

The Dark Comes Through Us

Midnight,
The shadows that watch us,
Through the autumn Aspens,
Blue Spruce,
And the Cottonwood,
There,
A full moon,
Casts a net,
Saturating,
The scent of light and dark,
Leaves,
And then the snow came,
Silent,
As midnight.

There Are No Bad Days When You're Fishing

Before the Sun,
I made twenty-four casts,
Into the black shadows,
Looking for swirls on the glass,
In the distance,
A heron screams,
He, like me,
Always searching,
The boat is in a perfect drift,
Taking me along the shoreline,
A fallen tree,
Rocks poking through,
Make for good targets,

The twenty-fifth cast,
I suck in air,
As the line goes tight,
The drag on my rod strains,
And complains,
The rush of adrenaline,
More powerful than drugs,
Then,
As fast as it comes,
It goes,
Lost or let go,
The fish,
Smarter than me,
Is left to be,

I continue to cast,
Listening for the geese,
As they get up from the water,
Like an alarm clock,
Letting me know,
I need to head home to work,
A cool crisp Fall morning,
There are no bad days,
When you're fishing.

The Lightning Bugs Will Emerge

Where do you go,
When you want to feel safe,
Escape the fear,
That creeps in,

What do you look for?
A solitary place?

Close your eyes,

Look to the sun,
Feel the warm sand,
Listen to the ocean,
Breathe in the salt air,

Drive east or west,
Roll down the window,
Turn the radio up,
Follow the setting or rising sun,

White lines,
A rhythm and a beat of time,

Stand barefooted in the grass,
Become grounded,
Hike a trail,
Take a walk,
Ride a bike,
See the nature,
See the sights,

Call me,
I can listen,
Tell me your troubles,
Send me your tears,
Sit on the porch,
We'll drink a few beers,

Study yourself,
Look inside,
Believe in the future,
In 100 years,
All your fears will be gone,
Your memory will be remembered,

That carefree feeling,
That left you in your youth,

That smile,
That made you feel happy,

When you we are alone,
And no one was home,

That laugh that was contagious,
That spread all around,
We all lose that feeling,
When we go to the ground,
Though you are not there yet,
No, far from it,

More mornings are in front of you,
A million or more,
Wake up and face it,
Open the door,
Expand your mind a little,
Let go of the unknown,
Meet me in the ether,
I will welcome you home.

Spiraling Equinox

There seems a long slow tide,
Drifting us out of the winter hide,
Discarding the layers of grit and grime,
Windy weather and frozen time,

There seems a long slow tide,
Drifting out a winter hide,
The gray and the gloom,
The ending soon,

There is a long slow tide,
Drifting us out, the winter hide,
The sickness and sinner's sake,
The redemption for us to make,

With March and April, a changing tide,
The Spring rebirth that coincides,
Blooms and buds,
Body and blood,

The March and April changing tide,
The Springs rebirth that coincides,
The taste of the sun upon our lips,
The feel of warmth as a postscript,

The depression of shorter days,
Gives way and clears the haze,
Each minute of extra light,
Give us forgiveness and makes us contrite,

There seems a long slow tide,
Breaking from the winter hide,
Pulling us toward the change of pace,
Leading us to goodness and grace.

Mind Full

It's like an old tune,
That gets stuck in your head,
While you are wandering,
It's like an old song,
That had meaning,
Years ago, in the past,
It's like an old pair of jeans,
That hold fit just right,
For a fortunate amount of time,
It's like an old lover,
That makes you smile,
On a cold winter's night,
It's like an old coffee mug,
That holds the liquid,
To wake you in the morning,
It's come to my attention,
That the past has past us,
Like a gravel road overgrown,
A school playground,
Rusted,
Like the wrinkles around your eyes,
When you smile,
At the warming sun.

Landlocked Sailing

Can't figure out,
How we got here,
Not that I know,
That I care,
Seven miles,
Off the coastline,
Floating on salt,
And air,
And you know,
And you know,
Anything that's out here,
Or nothing at all,
There's wind all around us,
There are ghosts in the sails,
Clearly, I see it,
The salt and the sea,
The map that holds magic,
The compass is key,
There's wind all around us,
There are ghosts in the sails,
How clearly, I see it,
The salt and the sea,
How long have we been out here?
How long till the Keys?
We followed the Gulf Stream,
We followed the dream,
And there is wind all around us,
There are ghosts in the sails,
There's no shade or shelter,
There's no guarantee,
That the wind all around us,
Will follow the dreams.

A New Day

A window opened,
A new day,

The sun peeked through the gray sky,
Giving us hope,

A daffodil bloomed,
A volunteer,
Moved by the warm weather,

A deep breath,
The smell of fresh cut grass,
After a dormant winter,

Robins magically appear,
A ray of hope,
A small splash of Spring,

And you can feel a little better,
Start to shed some fears,
Some anxiety,

A pair of shorts,
Paired with a sweatshirt,

A look in the closet,
To make sure your flip-flops are available,

A quick smile,
To yourself,
For yourself,

And find yourself,
Amidst all the negative,
Feeling fresh, positive,
And still alive.

October Fishing, A Full Moon

I stare at the Hunter Moon,
As it rises over the river and trees,
The last cast of the evening,
I dance the lure across the water,
The hope of a strike,
A bite,
From an unknowing rockfish,
The wind has died down,
A chill rises,
And reminds me,
To zip up my,
Fish blood and coffee stained,
Torn and tattered,
Carhartt,
The coffee,
Luke warm,
Sits alone at the stern of the boat,
Waiting to be drank or tossed,
The leaves on the trees,
Are forgiven,
As they turn from summer to fall,
One more cast,
Out of a hundred,
The moon winks on the water,
It is time to go home,
Putting the fishing rod away,
I start the engine,
And idle in,
Watching the lights,
Come on,
People coming home,
The scent of wood burning,

And a fine fog....smoke,
On the water,
A cormorant moves out of my way,
I leave a wake,
I traveled this river before,
Before the morning light,
After the sun has set,
And all the in-between,
Following my instinct and landmarks,
More than electronics,
Passing Buoys,
Passing time,
Time alone,
Time will tell,
Till tomorrow.

Wanderlust

We hiked the Appalachian Trail,
Lewis Falls,
Angels Rest,
McAffee Knob,
Around the Shenandoah,
Away from the city,
The Fall and Winter,
Are filled with solitude,
And forgiveness,
The vista and view,
The valley fog and dew,
Brings a calm and cold,
A new attitude,
High above an eagle soars,
In the distance a freight train,
Rumbles,
A faint echoing roar,
The climb,
The descent,
The sun flickers,
And away it went,
We drank water warm,
Along the way,
Listened to the cardinals sing,
Watched the chipmunks play,
Found Mother Nature,
With every gentle step,
Saw God's artwork,
When we got started,
Before we left.

Winter, Wind Chill
•••••••••••••••

The shadows,
Cast a lonely light,
The sunlight sprints,
Behind the horizons,
Like a thousand neon lights,
Blurred by the headlights,
The moon,
That came too soon,
Shuttled to the stars,
To the late-night dreams,
Hopes,
Promises,
Of today.

Swirls of Light

I watch the rain come down outside,
A cup of tea,
A cup of coffee,
A glass of water,
A glass of wine,
I watch,
As the rain turns from rain,
To snow,
And begins to swirl,
Cover the dark,
To light,
The gray,
The birds,
That flit and fly,
Among the winter.

Sleeping Under the Stars

The smell of fresh cut watermelon,
Waifs through the air,
Summertime,
Shorts, flip-flops,
Not a care,
The heat,
The humidity,
The sunshine,
The Bay ebbs and flows,
With a defined fluidity,
The smell of honeysuckle,
Waifs through the air,
Summertime,
Tan bodies, bleached hair,
Not a care,
The waves,
The salt,
The ocean in time and flow,
The smell of suntan lotion,
Waifs through the air,
Summertime,
Pools, creeks,
Not a care,
The thunderstorms,
The fresh grass and blossoming flowers,
The attitude of vacation throughout the season.

Elements
. . . .

I am but a blip on the radar,
You,
You are the ocean,
The scent of the salt and sea,
The feel of the sun and sand,
Embracing the earth,
With your soul.

Planet Earth From the Moon

Covered in clouds,
Like someone dropped cotton balls,
That have been torn up by a neighbor's cat,
Blue runs the Ocean,
Vast, as the setting sun,
I look down,
And wonder at the world,
Individuals are not seen,
There is only cause and effect,
The Chesapeake Bay,
The mighty Mississippi,
Look like spilt chocolate milk,
Running across the kitchen table,
This is the Earth,
This is not people,
This is not gun control,
This is not politicians,
This is not you,
This is not me,
This is the wind,
Then rain,
Day,
Night,
This is a blue marble from space,
This is one person,
Standing on the moon,
Hoping,
Wishing,
Praying,
Dreaming,
Down there,
Humanity,

And a kid that is gazing up at the moon,
Hoping,
Wishing,
Praying,
Dreaming,
"Star light, Star bright..."

Friday Night

Contrail's head into the western sky,
Like a road map,
Fading,
Orange and soft blues,
Mix into the evening sky,
I walk barefoot,
In the fresh cut grass,
Five years old,
Or 60,
A full moon rises,
As the sun sets,
The heat of the day,
Dissipates,
Like the work week,
It is Friday,
And the stress of the day,
Floats away,
Fades,
Like ice into a glass,
Tito's Vodka and lime,
And a dash of tonic.

CHAPTER 5

Miscellaneous

Vulnerable,

Worried,

Scared,

Confused,

We are,

You,

We are,

Me,

We are **US**,

The US,

We are Democrats,

We are Republicans,

"We the People",

We care,

We grieve,

We work,

We **fight**,

We want to **live**,

We want to be,

Free,

We are free,

We **worry** about parents,

Kids,

About **you**,

About the world,

We want it to be right,

We fear it might be wrong,

Listen,

Listen to what makes **you** feel right,

You are not wrong,

I am not right,

Listen to what is inside,

Believe in you,
Believe in me,
We are one,
We are one,
We are one,
Breath,
In,
Breathe,
Out,
A mask,
A minute,
A mile,
A moment,
Time,
Time will tell,
Time will pass,
Time will figure,
This all out,
Breathe in,
Breathe out.

Untitled
• • • • • • • •

You come to me,
With not a care,
Blonde and fun,
Running through your hair,
I'm to blame,
We are all here insane,
The morning coffee is way too hot,
Out of earshot,
Run with me,
Run with me,
Down to the angry sea,
See the waves,
Crashing in the haze,
In a million-mile stare,
Your lips are cold,
I don't care,
Truth be told,
Bring in the summer wind,
Come home soon,
The ceremony was nice,
Done by noon,
Left alone,
In my room.

Back in the Day...Tonight
· · · · · · · · · · · · · · · · · · · ·

The cassette plays,
"Thunder Road",
We didn't have social media back then,
We called a home phone,
We went out on a Friday or Saturday,
The world smelled like road trip gasoline,
Neon lights, open all night,
Ten bucks and a fill up,
We drive,
White lines,
Throwing beer bottles at the Speed limit signs,
The windows down,
A bench seat,
Keeps us close,
The speedometer reaches 90,
A roadie between my legs,
A full moon,
Tonight,
Was just yesterday,
There was a full moon,
And life was innocent,
McDonalds was okay,
7/11 had burritos and beer,
Radio stations kept us awake,
The rearview mirror was a memory,
And held us captive,
Sunday, we awoke,
Wondered where we had been,
And we begin again.

Mrs. Wallace died today,
All alone,
With no one home,
Lying in bed,
She passed away,
She had a fever,
She had a cough,
She had no one,
Around,
No family,
No friends,
No one to say goodbye to,
No one to hear her,
Her last breath of existence,

Mrs. Wallace died today,
As you ran outside,
Ran and played,
Shed no tears,
For a woman all alone,
With no one home,
Her phone was turned off months before,
No one came knocking at her door,
A virus, the flu,
A box of crackers,
And bills past due,

Mrs. Wallace died today,
Birthday cards of her 90th birthday,
Thrown away,
For a woman all alone,
With no one home,
A stray cat that came to her porch,

An empty food bowl,
With nothing to put forth,
The drip of water,
From the faucet sink,
We ran outside,
Not stopping to think,

Mrs. Wallace died today,
With a label of a virus,
Present day,
With no one home,
All alone,
A clock ticked,
In the living room,
No one will be here,
Soon,
Mrs. Wallace became an invisible number,
It's no wonder,
Mrs. Wallace died today.

Stay (a) Home

Clutter and chaos,
Media static,
Like Anne Frank,
Rummaging around in your attic,
Analog without Dialog,
We slip into solitude,
A different attitude,
Isolation,
Confirmation,
Deaths,
Tests,
Slowing down the sounds,
That is around,
A tumbleweed rolls through town,
It takes a lot of work to be happy,
When we are all down,
A little,
To make it last a little,
A bend in the curve,
Stuck somewhere,
Between here,
And the middle,
Step outside,
Out of the house,
The place we hide,
Take a deep breath,
Of fresh air,
Feel the sunshine,
If you dare,
Here to there,
A moment without a care,
March, April, May, June,

A new normal,
Coming soon,
No one ever,
Ever gets out alive,
So, enjoy the time you have,
Don't waste your time,
To criticize,
Listen to the lies,
Enjoy the blue,
With the cotton ball clouds and skies,
Stay at home,
Live,
And survive,
Tomorrow,
The next day,
The next day,
We will be free again,
And when,
That day comes,
I will meet you,
A kiss,
A hug,
Under the Sun.

Late Last Night
•••••••••••••

Late last night,
In the in-between,
I awoke,
To,
700 thousand strings,
That had become unstrung,
Life now,
In America,
Is not what it used to be,
The sounds of boys and girls,
With their American dreams,
Are about to become undone,
Unless we can,
Come back together,
Whether or not,
I am a Rep or a Dem,
We all are saints among the sin,
This trip,
 Is all of us,
And we are all in,
And we will begin,
Over again,
To travel to a new tune,
Waking up at dusk,
Drinking at noon,
The sweet taste,
Of coffee or tea,
The sweet smell,
Of honeysuckle,
And time,
Will tell.

'Round Here

Just around,
Just around the corner,
Round here,
I see we are near,
To dance,
To romance,
To walk,
To lay,
In the grass,
On the beach,
To stay,
In the sun,
To be one,
With the moon,
With you,
The dreams,
We ensue,
Come due,
Soon,
Around the corner,
Just around the corner,
Round,
Here,
We are near, no fear, no tears, no reason,
We are into the summer season,
Round here.

There's a Hole in Daddy's Heart (homage to John Prine)

The Monte Carlo,
Had a front bench seat,
So, my girlfriend could sit next to me,
We drank beer,
Throwing the empties,
At the shotgun marked speed limit signs,
We were reaching our twenties,
Doing eighty,

She got a phone call,
John Prine was playin',
At the VFW and pool hall,
And that was all they were sayin',
Gassed up the tuna boat,
Bought a pack of Camels,
Non- filters,
Cold Miller Lites,
Bottles,
And headed west on I-64,
Foot on the gas,
To the floor,

Had a cassette deck,
That only played Springsteen,
And out there in the sticks,
We got one radio station,
WRDU,
Out of Raleigh,
We drove two hours,
Stopping once to pee,
This was before cops,
Stop lettin' country folk be,

Got to that VFW,
Me and my girlfriend,
The Pagans were there,
Fifty or so,
I parked the Monte Carlo,
And they don't care,
Long hair,
Wallet chains,
Girlfriend never mentioned,
The motorcycle gang,

I moseyed up the bar,
Asked for two Miller Lites,
Got the death stare,
That would have sent some other,
Running into the night,
Did I say Lite,
I meant Bud,
Threw a 5 on the counter,
And became much wiser,

There was no warmup act,
When John came on,
The front of the stage was jam packed,
But it was just me and John,
My girlfriend,
Who I need to keep an eye on,
John played that night,
To 100 or so,
All left with holes in their heart,
And so it goes,

We got invented to a party,
At the Pagans place,
A night filled with cocaine,

And weed that was PCP laced,
Stuck around for a minute or two,
Allman Brothers blasting on the stereo,
Got the hell out of there, don't you know,

Drove thru the night,
White lines of I-64,
Girlfriends head in my lap,
Legs hanging out the door,
Prine's music,
Rattling around in my brain,
Who knows,
"Jesus Christ died for nothin, I suppose".

Springtime C-19 2020
● ● ● ● ● ● ● ● ● ● ● ● ● ● ●

Quarantine me,
In the warm waters of the Gulf Stream,
Vaccinate me,
With the pristine ocean so blue,
Intervene with me,
When all this C-19,
Has done its due,
Just quarantine me,
In the warm waters,
Of the Gulf Stream blue,

While we were quarantined,
It was unforeseen by me,
We'd run out of sunscreen for me,
As we floated on this dream,
With nothing between,
The just me and you,
Just quarantine me,
In the warm waters of the Gulf Stream.

Quarantine With Edgar Allen Poe's Ghost

Welcome,
To the night of sun,
Diluted, dilated eyes,
A Half past midnight,
And then some,
Shadows cast,
From looming oak trees,
Green grass from brown,
Come in we are open,
The friendship fast,
Music wafts around,
Bouncing off bookshelves,
In the air and on the ground,
Simple senses,
Eyesight,
Sound,
A dog barks,
Off in the distance,
The warmth of the fireplace,
Takes the chill from the room,
The book lays open, unread,
His wife upstairs, in bed,
Un-woken,
Tomorrow's troubles,
Set aside for the moment,
A peaceful dream,
No worries,
In a blissful moment,
A cup of tea,
Seeps and steams,
Sleep has been tendered,
The world outside,

Reality rendered,
The morning comes,
The night,
The night,
Has finally surrendered.

Radio distortion,
Radio silence,
Sunlight,
Star bright,
A million,
A billion,
One person,
One death,
Too many,
To pity,
A name,
A nurse,
A doctor,
No cure,
No sense,
Nonsense,
Non sequitur,
Listen,
Listen,
Your heartbeat,
Our heartbeat,
The county,
The city,
The town,
This is us,
This is you,
We all sacrifice,
Some more than others,
Front line,
Bottom line,
The men and women,
Exposed,

To help,
Another,
Stay inside,
Stay alive,
One day,
One week,
One month,
No time,
Out of time,
And here we are,
The here and the now.

The New World (Jack Kerouac's, On the Road)

Gravitate,
No handshake,
Shutdown borders,
TP hoarders,
Canceled games,
All the same,
In a panic,
There's no picnic,
We self distance,
For existence?
COVID-19,
Sight unseen,
Doctors,
Nurses,
Fighting curses,
Intubation,
All the nation,
Testing kits,
Here we sit,
Congress adjourns,
Nero fiddles...
The world burns.

As much as I'd like to,
As much as we have been,

Together the places,
Together the dream,

There is no space between us,
No spectrum unseen,

I am sensing the best of,
The best of our dream,

There is love all around us,
The love that exists,

Between love and our friendship,
Between hugs and the kiss,

There is love all around us,
There is love that exists,

Without you I am nothing,
Sand and the sea,

Your taste has a texture,
Smiles that are free,

Your eyes have a kindness,
Bright as the stars to me,

There is love all around us,
It's easy to see,

There is love that exists,
In the you and the me.

Maya
•••••

As much as I'd like to,
As much as we've been,
As much as we've seen together,
The space and the scene,
There is no space between us,
No spectrum unseen,
I am sensing the best of things,
Sand and the sunset,
The river and streams,
We got lost in the present,
Like a ghost in the machine.

Library
•••••••

Letters,
Black,
Engineered on paper,
White,
Straight lines and numbers,
Words to inform,
To entertain,
To enrich,
To dream,
To educate,
To escape,

Freedom,
To be free,
To immerse yourself,
In another time,
Another land,
Different people,
Cultures,
Ideas,
To travel,
Without leaving,
Your home,

Your mind,
Can be exercised,
Your mind,
Can be expanded,
Your mind,
Can create,
All from words,
Sentences,
Paragraphs,

Chapters,
A simple book,

Fingertips,
That touch the page,
Books read,
Memories fade,
A bookshelf,
A book bag,
Storing stories,
Short and long,
Storing poems,
That sing a song,

A book,
Simple,
Yet,
Complex,
To hold in your hand,
To feel the power,
To hear the inner voice,
Narration,
Words flowing,
Available, free.

Bones and Blood
• • • • • • • • • • • • •

We fell,
Amid the bones and blood,
The rocky road,
And the mud,
Scarred and scabbed,
Left for dead,
We fell,
Amid the happy and sad,
The fuel and the fire,
The ember glow,
We fell,
A long time ago,
Each day and each night,
We got up and began the fight,
Among the brick and mortar,
Next to the metal and mangled,
We go up,
Amid the vines that tangled,
We fought off the constant and cold,
The new and the old,
We fought off,
They do as you're told,
We woke up,
The dreams and desires,
In the muck and the mire.

Objects May Appear Larger

He looked back in the rear view,
Seeing the setting sun's glow,
He knew she had to move forward,
Back there was nowhere to go,
Fighting the incoming tide and wind,
Fighting every time, he was knocked down,
Even if he had to begin again,
Like walking in a bog or marsh,
Like living on water,
Salty and harsh,
He looked back in the rear view,
But only once,
Maybe twice,
He made up his mind,
Right there and then,
If he had to start over,
He'd start over and keep going,
Until he was there, with where and the winds.

On the Road to Kathmandu

• •

We smoked hash,
With the locals,
Sampled their homemade wine,
Breathed in the air,
Two steps at a time,
4600 feet above sea level,
Heads in the clouds,
Got as close to God,
As one possibly can,
And still be alive,

We smoked hash with the locals,
Prayed under the mountain,
At five fifty-five,
Ask God to protect us,
Forgive us our sins,
One step at a time,
We begin again,

We smoked hash with the locals,
Slept in tents under the stars,
Listen to the wind howl at night,
Dreamed of dreams from afar,
Lit incense,
Listened to wind chimes,
We smoked hash with the locals,
Drank their homemade wine.

Pirates
••••••

Pirates sail towards us,
In the mid of night,
Itching for a silvery sword fight,
Slashing through the cannon ball smoke,
Swinging from the mast in the moonlight,
Eye patches,
And pegged legged,
Rotten smile,
And tooth decay,
Rape and pillage,
Burn us down,
Quite the fairy tale,
Quite the dream,
Or so it seems,
I take on Black Beard,
I hear the others scream,
You see blood,
You see guts,
You pull the trigger,
The fired shot,
We stay on deck,
Fighting the fight, we fought,
Lost in battle,
Or so they thought,
We sail on,
We sail true,
Sails sailing in the wind,
Flag flowing full in the breeze,
We dream on,
Upon the open sea,
We dream on,
From sheets askew,

We dream on,
Me and you,
Swords and sheaths,
Pistols and belts,
Gold doubloons and silver,
Treasure map equals,
Wealth,
And to find it, equals,
Bad health.

Love
• • • •

When I met her,
And she met me,
The spark flew,
Down to earth,
Salt,
And,
Sea,
She kissed me,
I kissed her,
Woke from the dream,
Woke her too,
Drove for miles,
Windows down,
Mind a buzz,
Summer heat,
Melting hearts,
Asphalt streets,
Pavement pounding,
Underneath the sheets,
Down to the river,
Clothes askew,
Swam under the moonlight,
Laid in the morning dew,
The sun rose,
Turning night into day,
I met her,
And she met me,
We fell in love,
Salt to Sea.

The Summer is Not Over

I am sorry,
For leaving you,
All alone,
While I go out,
And search the night sky,
The Big Dipper to the north,
With the Space Station,
Reflecting off the Sun,
Orion's Belt has yet to show up,
But if you listen,
The radio plays,
Springsteen, "Screen door slams, Mary's dress
waves",
I melt,
You sleep,
The stars,
Fall from the sky,
Or disappear,
Into the morning,
I am sorry,
I am not holding your hand,
And we miss the chance to kiss,
A Summer time kiss,
Light breeze,
Warm,
Soft,
I am sorry.

Mother/Daughter

I look back,
Across my shoulder,
And see a mother and child,
Standing on a street corner,
Near a bus stop,
At the beginning of a field of corn,
By a grocery store,
Outside an apartment building,
Next to a car,
Anywhere America,
This mother and child are white,
Black,
Latino,
Asian,
This is my mother,
Your mother,
This is someone's mother,
She is looking away from me,
I cannot see her face,
She holds her child's hand,
I cannot tell if she is happy,
Sad,
Desperate,
Angry,
She holds the child's hand gently,
But with intent.

A Nation is Born
●●●●●●●●●●●●

A bloom explodes into the sky,
The colors,
Red, white and blue,
On this Fourth of July,
We stand,
As Americans,
Because it is our right,
Because it is right,
Those that fought for our freedom,
Our independence,
Symbolized simply,
By a flag...
Thirteen stripes,
50 stars,
One nation,
Under God,
Indivisible,
We are One,
We are together,
We are who we are,
Because we are Americans,
And will fight for that freedom,
To be the,
United States of America,
You and me,
Might be different,
But we are all Americans,
A bloom explodes in the sky,
On this Fourth of July.

Anywhere USA

I am not naive,
No,
Far from it,
About guns,
And bullets,
And life,
And,
Death,
From a stranger,
In a place,
That is now,
Outlined,
In yellow tape,
A trail of tears,
Of families,
That are no longer whole,
That become sound bites on the nightly news,
That only last,
Until the next tragedy,
No,
I am not naive,
To what is now,
The new normal,
No,
I am not naive,
I am saddened.

Step Outside, Tonight (homage to NASA, Neil Armstrong, and Astronauts)

The moon,
Waning Gibbous,
Lights up the sky,
Accompanied by the stars,
That comfort and guide us,
A man,
Takes a step,
Then two,
Looking up at the sky tonight,
I hear JFK's speech,
"We choose to go to the moon",
Always changing,
Pushing and pulling,
The tide,
How many navigators,
Have looked,
To the sky, the stars,
And the moon,
And found their way,
I look up to the moon,
And find my way.

Do Not Wish; Do
• • • • • • • • • • • •

She wants to take him surfing,
Because the waves are breaking at the point,
She wants to take him sailing,
She wants to leave in the morning,
At first light,
Clouds are forming on the horizon,
There is a storm coming soon,
She gets a morning buzz,
She wants to skinny dip,
At the full moon,
Never smoked those cigarettes,
Maybe inhaled a time or two,
Never did cocaine,
Nothing heavy like that,
Rather spend her time,
Dancing in the rain,
She wants to take him to the mountains,
Hike in quiet of the birds and trees,
Wants to dream about the future,
Always fighting to be free,
A little bird came to my window,
As I lay awake in the night,
Singing a sad song about the world and things,
Telling me she lost her fight,
The little bird,
Told me,
She lost her dreams,
Missed out on the waves,
The sailing,
The hikes,
The dreams,

She lost all of those,
And other things,
They talk at night,
While he lays in bed,
Him and her,
She wants to take him to heaven,
To the moon,
He dreamed that night,
He'd see her soon.

Notre-Dame de Paris

We weep,
But why,
The world weeps,
But why,
For history?
For a symbol?
Of Paris,
Of country,
That once was,
That is now gone,
After surviving so much,
A revolution,
Revolt,
A world war,
Over 800 years,
We weep,
But why,
The world weeps,
But why,
Fires and flames,
A spire that reaches to the heavens,
Now gone,
A landmark,
A landscape,
Partly gone, changed, vanished,
Like the world we now live in,
Minute by minute,
The world changes,
Our lives change,
Our view changes,
We throw away phones, tv's, landscapes, parks, trees,
idyllic views,

Old buildings of the past crumple or are torn down
for progress,
We throw away peoples' lives, reputations, behind a
new landscape of social media,
Your opinions no longer matter,
Discourse over religion and politics,
Gone,
Hiding behind the ether,
And yet this stone structure still partially stands,
A symbol of history, religion, architecture,
Of Paris,
Of France,
Of the world,
And yes we weep,
And yes the world weeps.

The Dimming of Democracy

With the world watching,
The Capital of the United States,
Was swarmed,
Unlawfully,
Unprecedented,
Sad,
Crazy,
Insane,
Incited,

Democracy,
Was under siege today,
Democracy is under water,
Democrats,
Republicans,
A Constitution,
Bending,
But not breaking,
We must breathe,
I cannot breathe,

A Democracy,
Fragile,
A Democracy and a Constitution,
That is meant to Unite the People,
Not divide,
Is this America?
Is this the United States of America?
Is this what Freedom looks like?

I am saddened for the US,
I am shocked as an American,
This is not America,
This is not Democracy.

State of Mind/Between the Two/A Love Story

(Dedicated to Scott and Sharon)

They sat in the back of the boat,
Surveying the world around them,
Time and tide were on their side,
Waves and wind,
Salt and sea,
Diamonds reflecting off the water,
Of possibilities,
They sailed,
The wind strong enough,
The sails puffed and pulled,
She fell asleep in his lap,
He smiled contently,
As they passed the time,
The clock stopped,
Freeing the mind,
They were coming home,
Wherever that might be,
Between the sky,
And between the sea,
She dreamed,
Mermaid dreams,
He drifted,
Pleasantly,
They sat in the back of boat,
Surveying the world around them,
Time and tide were on their side,
Waves and wind,
Salt and sea,
Diamonds reflecting off the water,
Of possibilities.

Eugene Martin's Last Day in the Low Country

Morning,
A cup of coffee,
and the morning newspaper,
The birds are chirping,
The ceiling fan groans,
Against the passing of time,
Moving the air enough not to notice,
Sausage gravy and buttered biscuits,
Mid-Summer afternoon,
On the front porch,
The sweat from a glass of sweet, iced tea,
Spills onto the table,
Cicadas are screaming,
And then are silent,
Then ramp up again,
After seventeen years,
They have a lot of catching up to do,
A half-eaten tomato sandwich, on white bread,
The evening,
The humidity and heat,
Have taken over the day,
But are getting ready to leave,
Like a dinner guests after dessert,
Off in the distance a lawn mower is
marking rows in the grass,
A vodka tonic replaces the iced tea and dinner,
The ice melts faster than a snowbird
on his way out of Florida,
Finally,
He gets up from his rocker,
Knees creaking and cracking,
From years of abuse and neglect,

It reminds him of his house,
With its peeling paint,
And a lifetime of secrets and songs,
He moves slowly through the house,
Remembering a late-night dance with his wife,
They made love, on a night like this,
The pillows and cushions on the sofa akimbo,
His knees laughing at him now,
A smile crosses his face,
A slow climb up the steps to his bedroom,
He climbs like the men on the summit of Everest,
He takes his time, because that is all he has,
The sheets and pillows are cool to the touch,
But only for a minute,
Outside the moon is on full display,
The windows are wide open,
A mockingbird, he knows will
sing through the night,
The cicadas are still going,
In different trees,
Indifferent,
Slowly,
He drifts off to sleep,
In the back of his mind,
He hears the thunder,
And hears the pattering of rain,
On the tin roof,
And slips deeper into sleep,
Dreaming of that late night dance.